What Men Are Saying *Seduction Poems:*

GW01459538

"OMG!!!! This is ‹ *worked like magic!'*

"wow... These rocked my life! Thanks!"   anon

"4 sure [the hypno poem] "sublimity" worked very well,she could not imagine getting such a poem, in that she went showing it off to her friends en they were 'like hey boy where did u get ya gal such a poem'en i was lyk frm a clean friend of mine.where am wrighting frm am frm KENYA in NAIROBI,ave a good time."   Cyrus

"My wife loves the poems and when I put her into a trance and read them to her I get Great results."
                                                    Bill

"Please can i have more of the poem thank you very much for that, it swept the feet of my baby girl."   Gabreal

"I read your poem to one woman who I haven't touched in years....She is literally begging me now since getting back in touch with me (bumped into each other at work and was still horny for me anyway,) but now even more so, she is practically dripping thru the phone as I read poems to her....(she thinks I write them). She said she let

What Women Are Saying About "Hypnopoetics..."
Hypnotic Seduction Poems:

*"I am a woman, and I used them with a man. I am
very pleased with the results. I read several of
them to him as I lay with my head in his lap..
reading softly and slowly, and gazing into his eyes
when ever I could without losing my place.
Watching his face go from 'but I wanted to watch
TV', to interest and then tenderness was awesome!
Thanks Phil for you poems, you newsletters, and
you book!"*   *Jen*

*"Phil, I wanted to tell you what a lovely, hypnotic
poem Sublimity is. It definitely draws your
imagination inward and puts you in that "special"
place where anything is possible. Thanks for
sharing,"*   *Cindy*

*"I have been meaning to email you to let you
know what has been happening since you helped
me with my last question, but i have been busy.
After reading to him for 3 nights in a row,
amazingly his behavior was "WOW" ... what a
change!! this man has stopped giving me affection
for almost a year, and suddenly he starts being the
affectionate man i met. So, I stopped reading, and
sure enough the attention stopped. Am i going
crazy? "*   *Sandra*

*"I used to think there is no point to buy new
poems- we have tons of great classics, why should
we pay for the work by somebody unknown?*

Phil's work gave me the answer: because they bring you a new pleasure you never imagined! His wording is elegantly sensual, and breathtaking - echoing like instruments in an orchestra that stimulate your imagination endlessly ..."
Kanae

"Thank you for these beautiful poems! I really feel the messages originate for your heart center and express the depth of such truths and beauty. You somehow summed up the deepest part of my emotions and feelings ... in ways that I myself had a hard time to verbalize. I read the poems and my heart is touched...thank you!" **Shuntena**

" I live in Jogjakarta but now i am in Lao for the job. Reading your poems can touch my soul deeply. You are so genius to fulfill your poems with soul and love, with your heart voices. Thanks again Phil, keep creating please..this world needs a guy like you. Cheers," **AE**

More testimonials from women at
www.hypnopoetics.com/testimonials-women.htm

Hypnopoetics…
Modern Love Poems and Hypnotic Inductions

Phil Billitz

www.hypnopoetics.com

www.hypnopoetics.com

Contents

Foreword...i
Ocean Sunset 1
Sublimity 3
Milonguero 5
Moment of Grace 7
Right Now 9
In an Instant 11
Clarity 13
Unvalentine..15
Manzana...17
The Difference 21
Coming to Love..23
Certainly 25
How Will I Know You? 27
Reciprocity 29
Touch 31
To Truly See 31
Lion and the Rose 35
Pegasus 37
Healing 39
Another Time...41
Locket...43

Foreword

Hypnosis Disguised as Poetry or Poetry Written Hypnotically?

Hypnotic poems are certainly not new. Since the beginning of time, some poetry has had a profoundly hypnotic effect. Its rhythm, meter, rhyme and cadence are such that its recitation has a mesmerizing effect. And certainly my favorite poems have always been those that capture and lead the imagination.

But, what would happen if one were to intentionally combine the language and technology of hypnosis and the language of poetry to produce a specific state of mind in the listener? Well, you would end up with this book.

I was trying to explain the poems in this book to a literary agent one day, and after describing them as best I could, I finally said: "Look, there is something you need to know about these poems. They are not really poems at all. They are hypnotic inductions that use the language of Hypnosis and Neuro-Linguistic Programming to program a woman's unconscious mind to make her fall hopelessly in love with you."

After looking at me, looking at the manuscript and looking back at me, all he could think of to say was, "Should I be creeped out by this?"

After I assured him that he would not be hypnotized and seduced if I were to read him some of them, I did so. His reaction was that he felt soothed and relaxed and not at all in love with me, but was intrigued and wanted to find out more.

i

So you, Dear Reader, may end up wondering the same thing. To answer that right away, no, you shouldn't feel creeped out at all. But you may find yourself feeling intrigued, captivated and motivated to read and understand them. And perhaps becoming interested in learning more about the language patterns and technology used in them.

Which brings us to an important point about hypnotism: hypnosis can only persuade a person to do what they were always willing to do in the first place. If you don't want to dance like a chicken, no hypnotic power on earth is going to get you scratching around in the dirt.

Hypnopoetics

Hypnopoetics works in a similar way. If a woman is totally closed to romance, or is physically repelled by your lack of hygiene, you are probably not going to get her to quickly and hopelessly fall in love with you - no matter how good the poems are.

However, the good news is that in general, women love romance and want to fall in love. And they need to experience a sense of connection before they can find a man attractive and become emotionally and physically involved with him.

This poetry will create the connection and the attraction will follow. And it creates that connection, and more, by using the science and language of Hypnosis and NLP.

Poetry Based on the New Science of Instant Behavior Change

Neuro-linguistic Programming (NLP) was created by Dr. John Grinder and Richard Bandler on the campus of the

University of California at Santa Cruz. Working together, the pair developed NLP - the most incredibly powerful change technology known to mankind.

Their books and techniques have helped thousands of people change their beliefs and their lives by overcoming Shyness, Procrastination, Fear and Doubt, Lack of Confidence, Test Anxiety, Fear of Public Speaking, and even get rid of the tragic effects of Childhood Trauma.

NLP produces powerful shifts in attitudes and behavior in a matter of minutes. People from all over the world studied their techniques because of their power to produce change. One of these students was Tony Robbins. Today, you see him on infomercials as the self-help guru of the world; but his roots are solidly based in NLP.

Bandler and Grinder invented techniques to model people who were experts in their field, and taught people how to achieve results just like the masters. And the techniques are often used in professional sports training programs. What would it be worth to have the golfing skills of Tiger Woods? What if you had the entrepreneurial drive of Bill Gates? What if you had the charisma of Mick Jagger?

One of the masters they modeled was Milton Erickson, probably the most famous and most effective hypnotist in the history of psychology. They studied and modeled his use of language to take people into and out of hypnotic trance, and to create immediate, dramatic changes in their beliefs and behavior just by talking to them.

The Use for NLP That They Don't Tell You About

There is another application for NLP that is equally as powerful as the ones above. But you won't read about it in many books because it is considered too controversial. Even the people that use it often don't admit that is what they are doing. It is the use of NLP for romance and seduction.

Because, falling in love is a process, a process in which someone moves through a series of mental and emotional states. And like any internal process, NLP can be used to model and reproduce its results, and to capture and lead the imagination in such a way as to speed up the process so that it can happen in a matter of minutes instead of months.

This poetry is written using these NLP techniques. It is designed to change a woman's state of mind in the right order and sequence to lead her to where she has always wanted to go, to fall deeply and completely in love. To give credit where it is due, the first poetry of this kind that I became aware of was written by Ross Jeffries.

Now, I don't want to try to train you in NLP or Ericksonian hypnosis - the point is that these technologies work. And better yet, they will work for you without knowing anything about either of these topics. That is the point of making these poems available to you - you don't have to know a thing about the technology. Simply start to use the poems and see the astounding results for yourself.

These poems can have a very powerful influence on the unconscious mind of the listener. How powerful is it? Think about falling deliriously in love in minutes instead of months. What if that could happen to you? Wouldn't you want to do that? Now?

Specifically, this beautiful poetry uses trance language, softeners, imbedded commands, tonality, universal experiences, Ericksonian hypnosis language patterns, covert communication techniques, and phonetic ambiguity. This powerful language is used in a way to evoke the process of falling in love, of increasing the passion and intensity of an existing relationship, to provide closure to the heart and soul after a relationship has ended.

These poems gently and gracefully change women's mental and emotional states to the state YOU desire without their awareness, and allow you to overcome resistance without argument, conflict or tension.

There is nothing unethical about using NLP to invite and lead someone into a closer relationship – people of both sexes are continually using cosmetics, clothing and fragrances to attract and keep love in their life. By using NLP, all you are doing, is simply creating the opportunity for them to experience that relationship in the most convincing, compelling, and psychologically-effective way possible.

And, of course, that gives you an incredible advantage over your competitors in this game of Love.

Phil Billitz
2012

Ocean Sunset

I don't know if you can imagine
looking out over the ocean
at a gorgeous sunset
the clouds glowing with an internal fire
that seems to be spreading on down
to the golden, molten, center of the sun.

And, as it sinks into the horizon
in the distance, on the beach
three friends walk along
the edge between water and world
at the junction of twilight and night.

Three gulls soar upward
lifted by the warm onshore breeze,
three waves in slow procession
wash away your thoughts of today –
replacing them with the memory
of two fingertips touching your face
your cheek touching
the cheek of your lover,
the sound as your lover breathes
two sighs gently into your ear.

Sighs so mysterious and slow
they enter and warm you
like the sunset's afterglow.
(cont.)

1

Two lovers falling gently asleep
in the safety of one another's arms:
one hope, one passion to inspire
one mind and one desire -
for me - these images
are origami unfolding
as you open your heart to me.

I wonder how much you will want to know me.
I wonder how much you will want to hold me.

Maybe you will give me
that lover's special gift; but
don't let yourself fall too quickly
try to resist for a moment or two
then just enjoy that slow intoxicating slide.

For you know when you allow yourself
to experience this moment
to feel your inhibitions melt away
you will start to notice
your feelings changing for me
like the sunset's spreading fire.

And, as you return from the world
of pleasure and dreams -
opening your eyes to your heart's desire.
can you see? Gently now,
one, two, three…

Sublimity

Can you remember a time
when fingertips touched your face
and the message that they traced was:
"How very precious you are to me"?

When you think of a love
that is all you could wish for
more than you expected
and all that you deserve;
when you wake in the morning
and lie warm in your bed
luxuriating in your body's memory
in that closeness and comfort
in that place of dreams
where memory and fantasy
and hopes combine -
in those first thoughts
you will find me there.

For, I have entered with these words
seeking sublime connection
to know you, and be known.

Can you remember a time
when fingertips touched your face?

Milonguero

Have you ever felt the magic
of a Tango connection
when held in a close embrace?

When the safety and power
of the lead's intention
sets your mind adrift someplace
and your movements become
the physical expression
of that beautiful smile on your face?

Have you ever felt your partner's
heart chakra open
when pressed against yours at the start
of a dance that you want
to last forever
and when it's over,
so reluctant to part
that you linger a moment
so impossible, so sweet…
then are swept away
by another, even better
dream that is moving your feet?

Can you let yourself fall
into a fairytale
a daydream, a reverie
(cont.)

www.hypnopoetics.com

where you allow yourself to believe
that miracles can happen
then open your heart to receive?

Can you come upon a time
when you suddenly know
someone will fill - your every need
as the magic in the music
is guiding your movements
by flowing into you through the lead?

Moment of Grace

Sometimes in an evening
there is a Tango moment
after a dance so dreamy and smooth -
the music has stopped but your embrace continues
and neither of you
is willing to move.

So, you stand together though the music has finished
and you feel that your heart is swelled
filled with those feelings of incredible connection
during the dance they continued to build.

Because for a time you were soaring
you floated you flew
through time, through the night,
through space until you knew
that souls can be coupled
that you are no longer alone
that you have found the connection
that has taken you home.

In your bodies you feel the music continue
both breathless in that close embrace
just heartbeats away from those wonderful
movements
in that lingering moment of grace;
'til your breathing is matched
(cont.)

to your partner's breath
and you focus on things unseen
on all of the places your bodies are touching
with no barriers,
no boundaries between.

Around you other couples have ended their dance
but neither of you is willing to release
this blissful moment of magical completion
with its sense of fullness and peace;
yet in that fullness you can feel
a yearning that you must satisfy
because the strength
that dwells in your heart
has given you this magic tonight.

Right Now

Have you ever seen the future
when you looked in someone's eyes?

It's as if you suddenly realize
that this was meant to be
as you feel yourself being drawn
oh, so willingly
into the warm embrace of their arms.

You really shouldn't, I know,
just let yourself go
and surrender to those feelings
But, what would it be like
if you choose to do this?

What would it feel like
to give yourself over
to that warm rush
of anticipation and pleasure
as you come
to this understanding,
as you open your heart to another heart
right now?

www.hypnopoetics.com

In an Instant

Have you ever experienced
instantaneous connection
with someone you hardly know?

Perhaps you feel it in a dance
or see it in a glance
or hear it in their voice –
but once you notice, you have no choice:
you feel the attraction growing
as if a band of energy is glowing
with the strength of the bond between you.

You see illumination, hear sublime communication
as the attraction binds and entwines you
and as you sit and talk
you mutually discover
the miracle, the wonder of each other.

So soft, so tender those thoughts
so passionate that connection
that you can just stop
and imagine a time
in the not far off or distant future
when you know you will be together
know that you have discovered
someone who wants to find you
someone who could be found.
(cont.)

But, first you must address
the universe and its possibilities
acknowledge that you are ready
accept that the time has come
to say yes to the moment
say yes to the stars
say yes to yourself and discover
the person you really are.

Clarity

A person can sometimes
see the future so clearly...

Have you ever met someone and suddenly
you can picture yourself with them
sometime in the future
laughing and sharing moments so sweet;
thinking back to today, remembering when
this fantastic connection began?

As you picture this
you can watch that image grow
to the point that you find yourself
dreaming a brighter tomorrow.

What is it like to imagine yourself
spending a timeless autumn afternoon
drifting in golden pleasure?

What would it feel like for you
to kiss them while illuminated
by the long warm rays of the sun?

It is not necessary for you to picture
all those intimate scenes -
you really shouldn't dream
of one morning waking to dawn in their arms.
(cont.)

But, when that flash of recognition occurs
– now –
it will seem as if
someone has appeared from nowhere
and you can see your life
is ready for a new direction.

You see things and people
from a different perspective -
and you watch the past's sad pictures
become dim and fade
as the bright scenes
of the two of us together
bring light to all the corners
and clarity to all the levels
of your exquisitely beautiful mind.

Unvalentine

If you will be my unvalentine
I promise you:
no romance, no drama
no urgency, no trauma
no quizzes, no tests
no greed, no need.

Instead we can share
long slow holding
sweet close breathing
whispered words and open talk
poetry, respect and honesty.

No rules, no roles
no pressure, sweet pleasure
just get to know me, and let me
learn to be your lover.

www.hypnopoetics.com

Manzana

Have you ever headed home
from a hard day at work
and all the way there you're thinking
you want nothing more than this:
a hot relaxing bath
or shower to soak in.

Maybe you imagine dropping
all your clothing and sliding
into that liquid pleasure
to soak away the tension
and fatigue of a rotten day.

Then comes that moment –
you're standing there
with steam rising from the tub
you can imagine the heat
working its way into you
imagine every part of your body
relaxing in warm release.

You pause to anticipate the feeling
then with a long and heartfelt sigh
you are sinking down
surrendering yourself completely
to the heat and relaxation.
(cont.)

Have you ever put aside
a special piece of chocolate
maybe a Ghirardelli or Godiva truffle
holding it back as a reward
for when you really need a lift?

It's always there in the back of your mind
and when you decide the time has come
– now – to unwrap it;
how you anticipate
the sweet revealing.

You might close your eyes
hold it right in front of your lips
as you pause and tease yourself
not quite touching it
savoring its dark aroma;
your lips open slightly
and there is the lightest touch of it
against your tongue
there is that first molecule of sweetness
then its richness fills your mouth.

Have you ever been attracted to someone
known that the attraction is mutual
even felt an incredible connection
and yet you hadn't acted on your feelings?

Then comes that moment
when the conversation stops
(cont.)

and you just look at each other knowing
that something is about to happen.

You begin to anticipate
that first electric kiss
that first soft brush of the lips
and whether you feel attraction's pull
bringing you together
or internal urges
pushing you into their arms;
suddenly you find you are kissing
and it's as if the waves of pleasure
contain all of the future pleasures
you now know that you will discover
and enjoy in this relationship
all wrapped up in that first
thrilling touch of a lover's lips.

The Difference

What is the difference
between what you think you want
what you have decided is
the best that you can have
and something that would truly fulfill you?

What is the difference
between what you expect to happen
what you have come to believe is possible
and something that would fill your life
with miracles and wonder?

Can you find that place within
where you don't need the approval of society
where it doesn't matter
what anyone else might think?

Can you find that place within
where you will decide to believe in this
to do this even though
it is like nothing you have believed
or done before?

And if you could have these things
if the choice were right in front of you – now,
how will you choose to choose it?
Now that you have chosen to do it?

Coming to Love

Coming to love is the process
of becoming who you already are –

Maybe you've been going along
with no love in your life
feeling ok, but somehow incomplete
then suddenly, everything changes
and life becomes so sweet.

You feel the pull of that attraction
are surprised by your own reactions
because you know the process has begun.

The more you think you can't
the more you realize you can
the longer you try to stall
the more you can feel yourself fall
until you just give in,
give yourself over to the moment.

For as soon as you say "yes"
you will feel the magical
and miraculous start to happen -
the magic that we all are looking for.

It starts as a feeling
(cont.)

an internal glimmer
that mirrors the sparkle
you see in a lover's eyes.

And the more you notice it
the stronger it gets
and the stronger it gets
the better it gets
and the better it gets
the better it gets
until you find yourself
saying their name out loud
you hear yourself
telling your friends about it
with that beautiful smile on your face.

Now – isn't that the way
you see yourself coming
now that you know
you are coming to love
and love is coming to you?

Certainly

On a certain day in a certain place
a certain woman was looking at a face
and suddenly
her life of uncertainty
became a memory.

For, as she looked at him she knew
something wonderful was coming true.

In the instant that it starts
she feels the beating of her heart
and perhaps the even better part
is to feel the glow in that spot
between her breasts
warmed as if by a gentle breath.

When she woke this morning
she knew in some mysterious way
that this new day
would be unlike any other;
and now she knows how;
every cell of her body knows, too
that she has deeply
and profoundly changed.

She had wondered
(cont.)

how she would enjoy
the warmth of a voice
the sparkle of his eyes;
now, she knows
how differently her body feels
whenever she is near him.

How the longing builds
the longing to be kissed
the way she likes to be kissed;
the longing to be held and loved
in the way she has always
wanted to be loved;
the longing to luxuriate
in the touch of skin to skin
to be illuminated from within
her radiant body
luminous with love.

So, "yes" she will say
"yes" in a way
she had never said "yes" before;
and of this she was certain
today she would open
and welcome him
in through that door.

How Will I Know You?

How will I know you when I find you
and how will you know me,
how will you show me
that you are beginning to be
mysteriously attracted to me?

A person is able to feel
that special connection
even at our first meeting -
that is how you feel
when you know that something is real.

You might try to resist
being drawn into my future
but, the fact that day is day and night is night
means that you might
be drawn from the darkness into a light.

A pure light that warms instead of burning
that begins at the center
of your being and spreads
all through your body
and your mind
and your heart until
you feel you never want to stop
the slow gentle drop
into the warm and liquid imagining.
(cont.)

Of a safe place where passion plays
and that wonderful smile stays
illuminating your face
as you fall into the grace
of love and knowledge
and belief in a love
beyond that which you remember
beyond that which you believed.

For you remember more
that you can know and know, too,
that you will remember this:
some day in the future
you are looking back at this moment
as the moment you fall
oh so helplessly
oh so willingly
into a spell of your own conjuring.

Now, feel the joy of finding out
that the thing you once looked for
that was misplaced and forgotten
that you despaired of ever finding again
once more has been found.

Reciprocity

When you are together,
laughter warms your heart
widens your smile
and the delight that you feel
is reflected in those eyes
that sparkle back at you.

When you breathe you can see
the chest of your lover rise and fall
in unison, in tempo, in time.

When you reach out you know
their arms are reaching out too;
when you touch them you feel
hands on your skin and when
you kiss them you know
that they are kissing you.

When your heart is ready to open
they are ready to enter
openly, honestly and then
when their energy flows into you
it is met, matched, and amplified
by the joy and love
flowing out from your center
transforming and transmuting
the lead of everyday experience
turning it into gold.

Touch

Have you ever felt yourself
longing for someone's touch
imagined their lips pressing on yours,
their memory resting
pleasantly in your mind?

Have you ever found yourself
filled with those feelings
so exciting -
of wanting to touch someone
and have your touch returned
because they fit so well in your life
and are planted so firmly
in that secret place in your heart -
because they awaken feelings inside you
that you had all but forgotten?

Can you remember that sudden rush
of desire when you finally held them
the rush that made you feel so alive:
your heartbeat quickly pounding
and your breathing
becoming ever deeper and faster?

If you are aware, as I am aware,
and as possible as I have learned to be
perhaps there is room still left in your heart
an opening in your life for me.

To Truly See

I have noticed you notice me
and wondered:
if you are the kind of person
who looks, then looks away;
or if you are someone
who can look and truly see.

For we look with our eyes,
but we see with our hearts
and when you find yourself
looking beyond the surface
you can see something deep inside
something that touches you deep inside.

Something ageless, timeless
and you know you are connecting
with that special place
where anything is possible
where anything can be tried on
that secret place
where daydreams become real
and wishes are fulfilled.

Should you find someone
in that place looking back
looking beyond the surface
that other people think is you;
(cont.)

33

When you feel connected in this way – now
you can stop and feel safe, but so excited;
feel secure, but with a longing, passion and desire
that lets you imagine a future
of happiness and pleasure
because you took a chance
and took the time to truly see.

Lion and the Rose

At first it had been curiosity
a sense of fascination and intrigue
that drew her to him
that pulled her into his world.

But then, the more she learned
the more she wanted to know
because the more she knew
the more she knew that she liked
the way he treated her
the way he made her feel.

And the stronger her feelings
the more she came – to understand –
that she had always wanted someone
mature enough to recognize
the woman she had become,
experienced enough to see
the woman she was coming to be.

Someone strong enough
to allow her to feel safe enough
to really let herself go
sensitive enough
so that she could let her feelings show.
(cont.)

Someone to take her to that place
where all things are possible,
where the rose is caressed by the lion
and the torrent of a waterfall plunges,
pounds deeply into a pool
of clear, warm, and fragrant waters.

Pegasus

She wanted to fly
to feel the strength and energy
of the love growing inside her
as she spreads her wings
and lifts to the sky.

She wanted to teach
the lessons that have no words
in a voice so eloquent
that it would heal all who heard it.

She wanted to touch
with the touch that knows no pressure,
knows only love's flow
through that purest, holiest of vessels.

And, she wanted to find
the bliss that sustains
because she had learned
that the kind of love that drains
can lead only to pain.

By now she could imagine
someone who would take her into his arms
where the strength of their passion
and their laughter would lift them up
as if they were each a wing
(cont.)

of some gentle but powerful being
that was using them
to soar through the sky
as they moved together as one, in unison.

And, they were fearless
never looking down because they knew
as surely as the universe sings
that even if their embrace should loosen
they would never be earthbound again –
even if Pegasus
should choose to fly alone.

Healing

What would it be like for you to find
that after such a long, long time
your heart is ready to trust
your soul is ready to heal
and your body is ready to feel those feelings
of hope and passion once again?

Can you imagine yourself placing your hand
on the knob of that door unopened,
where once you locked away
your dreams, fantasies and desire
where once you placed
those flickering embers of your heart
until you could welcome their fire?

When you know that you are ready now
to fill that space within
so that your long loneliness is finished
and your happiness can begin;
when you know that now you have finally found
someone with whom you can share
the peace and the passion
the warmth and the glow
that once again you feel beginning to grow
in that secret place, once hidden so well
now opening as if to the magic of a spell.

(cont.)

A person may not know
that you have already made that choice
until you hear something special
as you listen to a voice so close to your ear
with whispers that remove all your fear.

Because you know whatever happens
you have chosen to live
you have chosen to give
a priceless gift to yourself
the gift of loving once again.

Another Time

Have you ever loved
when you weren't supposed to care
when others try to say it's 'wrong'
but you know the love is there.

Friends and family might try to stop you
but your heart knows the truth
even if society doesn't understand
it's not a question of age or youth;
because the connection you feel
is certainly real
- now -
as you feel it happening to you.

Perhaps we were lovers
in some universe or another
or perhaps our souls met
in other bodies in another time –
it doesn't matter, for you know
this match is perfect
for your body and your mind.

Because now, you feel so connected
you feel so understood
and you know where this is headed
and you know it will be good…

Locket

My sweet and tender lover,
the time has come for us to part
as in our hearts
we both knew it would.

For reasons that neither of us can control
or begin to understand
we can no longer be together as we have been
in these extraordinary days.

And now, as you are leaving
there is one more understanding
that I want you to take
along with my love for you.

I have had the pleasure
and great good fortune to know you,
to discover the amazing woman
that you have kept hidden away;
I have had the privilege
to be the man to draw that woman
out into your life to stay.

I don't know if you can imagine
a locket, lying against your chest
where I have breathed my breath;
and in that locket you were to place
(cont.)

all our laughter, excitement,
all our pleasures
and the image of my face.

As that golden locket shuts
and closes on these wonder-filled days
imagine it down deep
close to your heart so with every beat
warm, true and strong it will keep.

And for all the times to come
when you feel lonely or afraid
when you feel a little down
when you just want to remember:

Reach in and with a touch so tender
rediscover the essence of all that is us
and everything we share
in that locket full of memories
because the images will still be there.

I can't begin to imagine
when or where or how
we will be able to meet again
to laugh and live as lovers can.

But until and unless we do
that locket full of thoughts
memories and feelings will stay with you:
the only remnant of this time,
(cont.)

like the warm coals that glow
after the blaze is burning low.

To the universe and to you
I give my thanks:
for our love is an amazing thing
something rare and wonderful
that has had its time.

And, this I know
and always it will be true:
you are more than I expected
all I ever wanted
and my life will be less without you.

The End

www.hypnopoetics.com

Dr. Richard G. Butler PhD, DD on "Hypnopoetics...Modern Love Poems and Hypnotic Inductions"

"Women, in general, are very open to poetic language in the first place, so they are already conditioned to receive an undertone of erotic and sensual messages ..."

"Women accept them because of their unobtrusive and romantic nature, without realizing the deep hidden commands that are taking place ..."

"I have noticed how positively and seductively they can work on a woman's psyche until she is totally enamored ... Just the other evening I had a woman wanting me so terribly ..."

"I might have been skeptical at first, had I not known from personal experience the powerful affects that NLP has on the listener."

"I am absolutely convinced that this beautiful technique works, being a writer of love and sensual poetry anyway, and to use these techniques only firmly cements the intentions deeper into the woman's subconscious mind, that she doesn't realize what is happening, and it is happening nonetheless ..."

"They are amazing, and so much fun to read as well, which is another factor that adds to the subliminal message ..."

"... thank you very much for your wonderful work of poetry. I will certainly have a great time reading it, and sharing it with my lady friends ..."

Richard G. Butler PhD, DD

At Amazon.com in the Kindle Store:

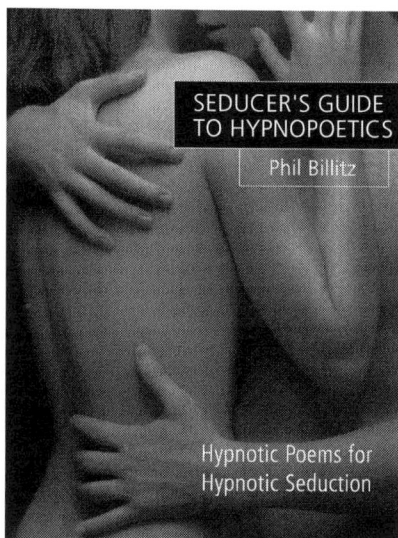

"The Seducer's Guide to Hypnopoetics"
Phil Billitz
http://www.amazon.com/dp/B007RI7HL8

The "Seducer's Guide to Hypnopoetics" is the Owner's Manual and
Instruction book for "Hypnopoetics...Modern Love Poems and
Hypnotic Inductions".

It tells you how and when to use the Hypnotic Seduction Poems (Hypno
Poems) in "Hypnopoetics..." and also discusses in detail the structure of
the Hypno Poems and how to write your own Hypnotic Seduction
Poetry.

Hypno Poems are especially useful for men who want to use NLP or
'Speed Seduction" ™ to pick up and seduce women without any
training or having to memorize 'patterns'.

Hypno Poems are easy to read and use, and the Seducer's Guide will
assist you in getting the maximum benefit from these powerful
Hypnotic Seduction Poems.

In Closing

As a purchaser of my book, you are entitled to receive invitations to teleseminars, updates to the eBook, bonuses and other useful information relating to Hypnotic Seduction.

In order for me to send these to you, I need your name and email address. So, please go to the following web address and sign up:

http://www.hypnopoetics.com/A-list-sign-up.html

Thanks,
Phil

3493683R00035

Printed in Great Britain
by Amazon.co.uk, Ltd.,
Marston Gate.